LOVE

OF YOUR LIFE

YOUR GUIDE TO FINDING AND RECOGNISING
YOUR SOULMATE

by

Siobhan Coulter

DEDICATION

I dedicate this book to Infinite Love and my soulmate Nick. Thank you for always shining so brightly in my life, leading me home to the infinite potentials that lie within me. Thank you for saying yes to Love over and over again. To infinity and beyond my love, together, always and forever in-Love.

And so it is.

THE AUTHOR

SIOBHAN COULTER

Siobhan Coulter guides individuals and couples on their journey toward discovering and embracing True Love. Her expertise spans psychology and the intuitive arts, harmoniously blending conventional understanding and universal wisdom. More than just a guide, Siobhan empowers individuals to cultivate and nurture profound connections capable of enduring the tests of time. Enriched by her profound experience of a 30-year partnership, Siobhan stands as an inspiring figure, offering guidance for every relationship stage.

Siobhan's insights transcend the ordinary and resonate with a deep understanding of the complexities of the soul, leaving an indelible imprint of wisdom, self-discovery and Infinite Love.

Namaste

You are the Love you seek

TABLE OF CONTENTS

INTRODUCTION

Manifestation is the process of deliberate creation. Where you change your life by bringing things into your life or sphere of reality. Things like people, soulmates, friends, food, health, abundance, money, jobs, travel, opportunities and of course Love.

Manifestation operates under the universal Law of Attraction which underpins our entire existence. The Law of Attraction dictates that you will receive more of what you already hold, and since it operates at an energetic level, your energy is the biggest indicator of what your manifestation results will be.

To successfully manifest your soulmate, every step of your manifestation process is required to be energetically empowered by the highest possible energy of love. That is: Infinite Love, which is the very desire that fuels your manifestation. That's right, your energy awareness is the game changer you have been waiting for.

Why is your energy so important? Because if you manifest in the right energy and maintain that energy, you will successfully manifest what you actually want, much faster than you expected plus you will feel amazing during the whole process.

To maximize your manifestation success, this book is divided into two sections:

Section One: Shares what needs to happen energetically *before* you consciously manifest your soulmate. If you follow the energetic empowerment process, you will save yourself a lot of time and heartache. If you already have a manifestation process in place and haven't received the results you desire, I recommend you put it aside and restart using the following guidance.

Section Two: Ensures your manifestation success with a *practical* step by step guide through the process and beyond with some maintenance tips.

That's right you won't just know what to do, you will also be guided every step of the way. Why? Because I care and I want you to succeed in your soulmate manifestation. I hope you will feel safe, supported and loved throughout this entire process. Now let's get started.

SECTION ONE

DECODING THE ENERGETIC EMPOWERMENT

OF CONSCIOUS MANIFESTATION

IAM: THE ESSENCE OF MANIFESTATION

Many people follow the IAM manifestation process which is essentially:

Intention + Action = Manifestation.

The definitions being:

I - Intention - Set your manifestation intentions for what you want

A - Action - Take purposeful action everyday to help your manifestations come to life

M - Manifest - Your manifestation physically appears in your life

The IAM process rightfully proposes that manifestations result as a direct consequence of intention setting and purposeful action. The

IAM process is what we all do, consciously and unconsciously, in every moment. The results of which appear to be random results that constitute our lived experience or reality.

Ever wonder why we don't always get what we want? It's not that you are doing it "wrong" , rather you may not have the energetic awareness and therefore the energetic alignment to deliver the results you want and truly deserve.

The IAM process works absolutely but we are not usually in the energy of what we want. We are in the energy of what we don't have. Therefore, the essential foundation for energetically empowering your manifesting and having a great love life is the awareness that:

The energy you hold is EVERYTHING.

HOW ENERGETIC EMPOWERMENT IMPACTS YOUR MANIFESTATIONS

Your manifestations are fueled or powered by the energy you hold. There is a big difference in setting your intentions with different energy levels, what is also known as *energetic alignment*. Aligning to the highest possible frequency of what you want obviously provides the best energy for you to set your intentions, which in turn positively impacts your manifestation results. Maintaining the highest possible energy whilst you wait for your manifestation outcomes, empowers your manifestation process right to its natural conclusion where you get the results you truly desire. Alignment to and maintaining lower frequencies, does not.

So what is the 'right' energy for manifesting your soulmate and a life together of everlasting Love? It's simple really, even if you don't know anything about energy. Instead of thinking energy, think *emotion*. Your feelings are your best indicator of the energy you hold and therefore your energy alignment. Feeling high and happy? Then your energy is good. Feeling tired, low and frustrated? Then your energy is low.

Simple but very powerful because you can generally change your energetic alignment depending on what you are thinking and talking about. Furthermore, thinking creates feelings which are often associated with physiological changes too.

Let's do an experiment:

Think about sucking on a really tart slice of lemon. Think about picking the lemon up, putting it to your mouth, sucking on it and tasting that tart, sour juice.

What happened for you?:

Did your mouth become dry or did you start to salivate? Did you feel a little apprehensive once you knew it was really tart? Did you taste the juice in your mouth?

Physiological and emotional changes can be subtle but your emotions and body (and therefore your energy) are always adapting to your thoughts.

In short, these are aspects of Cognitive Theory which state that cognitions including thoughts create emotional and physiological responses within our bodies (1). Our bodies change when we focus on different stimuli, like watching a baby sleep or a big pile of work being dumped on your desk. We are all familiar with the emotional and physical impacts of stress. Simply put, stress can feel heavy and low.

The good news is that whilst we can make ourselves feel low, we can also make ourselves feel good. Like focusing on getting a big hug from your favorite person, making love, eating your favorite dish, laughing with your friends, remembering feeling completely loved when you were young, even playing with your pet. Your favorite moments can make you feel better and raise your energy levels.

For you to successfully manifest your soulmate, each step in the manifestation process needs to be energetically empowered by Infinite Love. When we empower each step with Infinite Love, they become the *keys* which unlocking your soulmate manifestation.

1. DELIBERATE ENERGETIC ALIGNMENT

The science of Cognitive Theory only takes into account physiological and emotional states. From an enlightened perspective, we understand the impact goes much further, flowing to our body, mind and spirit; impacting our energy alignment to our Higher Self, the universe and all that is. Furthermore, our thoughts directly impact our energetic alignment to Source Energy or if you prefer Oneness, Goddess, or The Divine Creator. Please substitute whatever term you prefer.

Thinking thoughts that create good emotions within you, increases your energy alignment to 'good or lighter' energy. The more you continue having good thoughts and feelings, the higher your energy level rises. Start thinking about gratitude, kindness, hope, inspiration, expansion and Love… and you will really take your energy to higher levels. In the beginning, you might feel like you have to force yourself to think differently (and you do), but once you get going, the flow of good emotion tends to perpetuate itself so it becomes easier to do. With practice, it will feel effortless and easy, fun and enjoyable.

DELIBERATE ENERGETIC ALIGNMENT TO INFINITE LOVE

The deliberate alignment to Infinite Love requires a very deliberate choice:

Do you or do you not, choose Love?

Are you willing to Love again? 100%? All of you, with no games, resistance or hiding?

To be willing to give yourself to LOVE 100%? Not to another person, but to *Love*.

To choose Love even though you might get hurt, even though you might lose it, even though they might not love you back? Do you want to live a life of Love, even if you are the only one being loving? Do you believe in Love?

That's right, you are being asked to put down all your negative associations about Love, all your hurts, traumas, memories, vows, resistance and anger and choose Love again. How you release yourself from these memories can take time but an underlying choice for Love needs to be made NOW.

I urge you to choose Love, the highest Love possible. You deserve the very best.

To be the very best. To be who you truly are.

If yes, then choose how Love is going to be in your life. Let yourself day dream about the best possible Love Life you could ever have, now increase it by 100%, then another 100% and another, and so on. Yes, you can have it all. Yes, you *can* live a life of constant Love.

Yes, you can have all your dreams come true.

A great love life is different for everyone, what's yours? Now is the time to really think about it. Is it full of compassion, kindness, patience, inspiration, passion, laughter, joy, wisdom, growth, expansion, hope, abundance, cuddles, love, intimacy, goodness, grace or peace? All of the above and more? Day dream and find your ideal Love Life of Infinite Love.

Once you have a clear picture or at least a clearer emotional understanding of your best ever love life with your soulmate, metaphorically draw a line in your life between what has gone before and what will be from now on. Make a commitment to yourself that this is the only Love Life you will accept moving forward. This is now your new *Love Standard* and you will only engage with Love and potential partners who are resonating at this new Love Standard or above.

2. CONSCIOUS EMBODIMENT OF INFINITE LOVE

The next essential key to successfully manifesting your soulmate is to live or *embody* the emotional experience of already being In-love and your soulmate is already present in your life. Yes, that's right, let yourself become giddy with the feelings of being In-love.

This energetic manifestation key is known as Embodying Infinite Love.

Embodying Infinite Love is where alignment is taken a step further by you becoming Infinite Love. That is, you live, breathe, feel and embrace Infinite Love every day, as much as possible.

Once you feel your energy alignment is to Infinite Love, take it to an even higher level for your manifestation purposes. If you want to manifest your soulmate and live a life of Infinite happiness and Love, then take yourself to those feelings. Essentially, the energy alignment you are seeking is the emotional state you anticipate feeling when your soulmate is *already* in your life.

"But... how do I align and embody Infinite Love when I haven't met my soulmate yet?" I hear you ask. Don't worry, you'll be guided through the process in Section 2. In the meantime, remember you have to be holding the energy of having it already, in order to receive more.

So far we have covered two essential manifestation keys that energetically empower all successful Love manifestations, the deliberate alignment and conscious embodiment of Infinite Love. Both are required in establishing the highest energetic foundations for setting manifestation intentions. So that is the next key: Intention setting whilst embodying Infinite Love.

3. INTENTION SETTING WITH INFINITE LOVE

Intention setting is where you write down all your hopes, dreams and desires for your love life. Writing it down is a beautiful part of the process because it is where your intentions begin to take physical form, through your *own handwriting*. Don't type it, use a pen or pencil and write it down on paper. We will cover the specifics of what to intend for in more detail in Section Two.

The *purer and less complicated* your intentions are, the more effective they will be.

Intentions such as:

"I want to manifest my soulmate because I want to have a partner and children to love" are loaded with conditions and unnecessary complications.

Try to avoid statements that include 'because' and reasons why you want something, as they hold the energy of "not having love" and will only bring more of that energy.

A purer intention could be:

- I flow everyday with Infinite Love

- My family is growing through Infinite Love

- Love feels so good, so right. It's ever expanding in my life

- The love, trust and intimacy that I share with my soulmate is beyond my wildest expectations

- I love being Love. My life is amazing

Importantly, the more emotive you become whilst intention setting the better your results will be, as your emotions are directly linked to your energetic magnetism. The higher the emotion of love, gratitude, hope, inspiration etc you feel, the greater the magnetic pull will be felt by your soulmate.

To be very clear:

If you *desire*, *want* or *need* a relationship, you won't manifest your soulmate because the energy alignment is to 'not having'. Any relationships that do arise will not be permanent, easy or fun.

If you feel so completely loved everyday and know in every cell of your body that you have an amazing relationship with yourself and your soulmate, then the energy alignment is to gratefully having; joy; bliss; loved. Only your soulmate is contracted to create this with you, so of course they will find you soon.

4. OPEN FULLY AND RECEIVE LOVE

Since we live in a dimension that includes time and conscious creation, especially free will (both yours and your soulmates), most manifestations are not instantaneous and require time. Therefore daily maintenance of your alignment and embodiment of Infinite Love is the next essential key.

Imagine if you lit a bonfire for your soulmate to find you in the dark. They see it and start traveling towards you but you don't keep replenishing the logs on the bonfire. Soon it will die down and maybe even go out which makes it almost impossible for them to find you. Furthermore, thoughts of doubt and fear are like throwing buckets of water onto the fire. So make your bonfire bigger and brighter than you ever thought possible and tend to it everyday. Make it so strong and powerful that you will light up the fastest and easiest route for your soulmate to find you.

This manifestation key is linked to taking purposeful action in the IAM process. One of your actions is to keep opening up to more Love by embodying the perspective that you are constantly giving and receiving Love. This action will make it easier for your soulmate to find you. When you consistently and completely immerse yourself in the feelings of being completely BLISSED OUT IN-LOVE, you raise your entire energetic vibration and frequency. Imagine that it's no longer a bonfire but an energetic pulse that you are now constantly emitting from yourself. I like to call it your *Love Signature.* Not only is your Love Signature registering throughout the entire universe and universal consciousness of all beings, it is reaching across the planet and into the energy field of your soulmate and other True Love potentials with which you have soul contracts.

Your Love Signature signals to them that you are constantly vibrating with the highest energy of Infinite Love and have now reached your agreed upon frequency for them to find you. Essentially, you are now *energetically prepared for them, as per your soul contract.* The stronger you radiate such high feelings of love each day, the stronger your Love Signature is felt by your soulmate and True Love potentials, making it easier for them to be drawn to you.

Your Love Signature also communicates all of your manifestation intentions. That is, everything on your handwritten list, all your heart's desires about love, the frequency and purity of the love you hold and the relationship you want. Importantly, only vibrational matches to the energy you are emitting will be triggered by your Love Signature and begin to move towards you both energetically and physically. Whatever energy you hold, you will attract its vibrational match into your life. So it is key to keep radiating the highest vibrations and feelings of Love each day. This will draw your best vibrational matches to you, including your soulmate.

Receiving Love during this period can not be stressed enough. It's a mindset that you can easily cultivate by maintaining your alignment and embodiment of Infinite Love. Since it feels so good to do, it's actually really easy. Use affirmations, music, actions, self-pleasure, whatever you do through self-love and self-care to keep your alignment and embodiment. Then live your day in that energy and consciously receive Love from everything: the air, cloud, trees, people, food. Start to see that everything in your life is Love coming to you from Source Energy. The pavement you are walking on was laid for *you* (acknowledge and receive it); the street tree was planted to give *you* shade and connection to nature (acknowledge and receive it); the apple you are eating was grown to nourish *you* with love and nutrients (acknowledge and receive it); the flowers on the bushes are blooming just for *you* (acknowledge and receive it). And so on.

The awareness shift that you are consciously *receiving Infinite Love* is essential because it balances out your Love Life and sends a strong message to the universe that you are not just a huge giver of Love but you also receive all the Love energy being sent to you. You are now receiving Love unconditionally and in abundance. For many this will be a huge shift in your life, congratulations and enjoy all the different aspects of Love that are now coming to you into your life.

Energetically, consciously receiving Love creates an *incredibly strong portal or vacuum* within your heart chakra, where once activated you start pulling in more and more Love. It increases your magnetic pull through the Law of Attraction. Naturally your soulmate and True Love Potentials will feel it strongly as you are creating the fastest and easiest route for them to find you.

Consciously receiving Infinite Love 'feeds' your Love Portal, keeping it open and magnetically pulling your soulmate to you. It is amazing and when you are truly high In-Love you may even be able to feel it physically around your chest. You can consciously expand it by focusing on that feeling and feeling more Love. Imagine that it is widening and encompassing your whole chest, even your whole body. You will feel amazing as you bliss out In-Love.

5. YOU ARE THE LOVE YOU SEEK

As you continue to embody Infinite Love everyday, something magical begins to happen, you start to awaken further into more of who you truly are.

As you continue to be Blissed Out In-Love everyday feeling radiantly happy, with a magnetic Love Portal active with your heart, you actually *become* blissfully happy and content. It is an emotional place where you truly enjoy feeling In-love and consciously choose to feel In-love simply because it feels so good.

It is at this time that two realizations begin to dawn within you. Firstly, that you would prefer to be without a partner, if it meant compromising your current level of Love and contentment. Secondly, you are so blissfully happy that you would be ok if you never found your soulmate. In fact, you may realize that you have not been that focused on manifesting your soulmate for a few weeks. Besides, you feel so amazingly happy, how could life possibly get any better, even with your soulmate? Yes you read correctly, your yearning for your soulmate may be fading, yet you are blissfully happy and content. How could this be?

You have now reached a powerful and significant gateway in your ascension journey. You are discovering that:

Manifesting your soulmate was NEVER your ultimate goal. (play dramatic music here as you reread this sentence)

Your realisation that you truly enjoy giving and receiving Love everyday combined with your actualisation of prioritising your In-Love energy over lesser energies, was actually the outcome your Highest Self was leading you too:

The self-realisation and self-actualisation that you are the energy of Unconditional Love.

THE TRUE PURPOSE OF YOUR SOULMATE MANIFESTATION

That's right, manifesting your soulmate was never the ultimate goal of your Higher Self. Your innate desire for your soulmate was only the trigger for you to evolve into a Higher Frequency Being of Love, thus becoming more of your Highest Self. When you make a conscious choice that you truly love feeling this way and you no longer care if you find your soulmate, that is the moment that you truly free yourself from old beliefs patterns and third dimensional constraints of Love.

This realisation releases you to become more of who you truly are. Congratulations you are progressing well in your ascension journey!

When you reach this level, you are able to comprehend that you:

- are no longer tethered to conditional love that inevitably brings feelings of hurt and failure - AND you prefer to be unconditionally accepting with no expectations or judgements.

- are not dependent on anyone or anything to have Love and happiness - AND you freely give and receive love with joy.

- that the Love within you is enough - AND you truly believe it.

- that you have all the Love WITHIN you that you will ever need or want - AND you feel deeply contented and safe whilst also feeling inspired, expansive and creative.

- that you love being Loving and you proiritise your LOVING BEINGNESS over lesser energy states - AND you witness yourself being more of the person you want to be.

When Love becomes unconditional as to whether or not you have a partner, ironically that is when your soulmate will turn up physically in your life. That's right, when you truly don't need them, they turn up. Why? So that you can enjoy them and create a new type of relationship. A relationship founded in unconditional, Infinite Love. It will be unique, spectacular and a true gift to this world. So good, right? More on True Love Relationships a little later.

6. WHY? IT'S ALWAYS BEEN ABOUT YOU

Traditionally, the ascension path is taken on one of two routes. Firstly, to give up everything and isolate yourself. To go within through prayer, meditation or silent contemplation. Usually somewhere remote and in nature or within a religious organization where you give up marriage, children and devote your life to the Divine Creator (use your term here) through a life of service to others. Think monks, priests, nuns, yogis etc. The first route is considered easier because you remove yourself from the drama and distractions of daily life. This path has its own unique hardships and joys, as you can imagine.

The second route is through the household role, through relationships and using our connection to others to reveal our ultimate connection with yourself and to the Divine Creator (again, use your term here). The second route is considered harder because you remain within the drama and distractions of life. You also have to contend with free will (yours and especially others). Through the second route, ascension is found through relationships and connections. It is also the route where Tantra emerged as a process to find bliss through sacred sexuality. Guess which path you have chosen?

Your journey to find love and to have a loving partner has therefore *always been about you* and your ascension journey. Your burning desire to find love despite previous heartbreak is to assist you to self-realise *and* self-actualise: To become more of who you truly are.

One significant realisation on the ascension path is:

- the love you seek and the partnership you yearn for, does not exist outside of you. (Please pause and let that sink in for a while...)

THE SIGNIFICANCE OF RELATIONSHIPS

Every relationship you have ever had has always been trying to show you something about yourself that you have not yet faced or are willing to see. Every heartbreak has been an opportunity to release conditional love, upgrade to unconditional love and to rise above the drama and gracefully clear your karma. Every relationship has been an opportunity for you to discover the best version of yourself.

Every relationship you have ever had has been leading you *towards* love, not away from it.

Do not harbor resentment to past partners that were not your soulmate. That's like being angry at a potato for not being a carrot. They couldn't be a carrot if they tried. It's not their fault that you mistook them for a carrot. They were just helping you understand that you can't make a potato, a carrot. It's time, let it go.

Remember, the Law of Attraction dictates that you can not receive anything you do not already have. It's the Law.

When you realise:

- that *you are Love*,

- that *you* are the love and the relationship you have been seeking, and

- your love is *enough* to live an amazingly joyous, loving, contented, inspired life, then

you are exactly where your Higher Self was guiding you: to your I AM consciousness. Also known as your Creator Self, flowing with the energy that creates life.

All your relationships will begin to shift because your consciousness has shifted. Don't expect others to have changed, that is not how it works. You can not change others and they can not change you. Use your new found Beingness to change your behaviour, to love and accept them unconditionally. You will be amazed at how differently you will feel about your relationships. Maybe now, you can let it go. Maybe now, you will find the ascension gift that is held within each relationship. Ascension Gifts are only found through unconditional love, acceptance and contentment. You will know it when you find it, as it will unlock a joyous awareness within you that enlightens your wisdom and propels you forwards on your ascension path.

Remember: You are the creator of your life. You get to choose how you live. With Love or without Love. The choice has always been in your heart. It is not outside of you. Everything you seek is within you, therefore you hold the key to becoming who you truly desire to be.

The time has come.

You are ready.

You are loved, supported and it is safe. You can do this.

You are not alone. You have the entire support of the universe.

It is your destiny to do this.

So make your choice, open your heart completely and say 'yes' to Love.

SECTION TWO

BLISSED OUT IN-LOVE

This section will guide your soulmate manifestation by practically increasing your energetic alignment and embodiment of Infinite Love. Thus empowering your manifestation that will bring your soulmate to you. Often, when lots of words are given, it can be difficult to put them into practice. Especially when we are moving from thinking to feeling, both emotionally and physically.

Specifically, section two aims to help you empower your manifestation by reaching the best manifesting emotional state by guiding you to change how you feel. The texts are written to move you from a familiar feeling state to a lighter, more expansive state. As you read, really immerse yourself in your emotions and let yourself feel differently. If you can't feel something that is being described, don't give up. You can do this if you persist, so stay in that section for a little while and re-read that section. Maybe you need to stay with that section for a few minutes, hours, days or even a week. How long, doesn't matter. What matters is that you reach that feeling state being described in that section.

21

I like to call the feeling state we are aiming for:

BLISSED OUT IN-LOVE.

I am sure you will remember it once you get going. It is a process, so please participate all the way to the end as every step is essential for manifesting your soulmate and living a life of everlasting love and happiness together.

Each section is written to inspire you to connect deeply with Infinite Love, but for some individuals my words may not be the only way to get there. I encourage you to find your own words, if the text doesn't suit you, or you want to go further. What is important is that you reach that feeling of Blissed out In-Love. There are many paths available to you, find the one that is the most fun and accessible for you.

MANIFESTING: FROM VOWELS TO VOWS

Lucky for us, we have a string of English vowels to help remind us of what to do. Remember, AEIOU and sometimes Y?

The vowels will act similar to an acronym, as your guide to embody the essential manifestation keys into manifesting your soulmate. It will be an energetically empowered like no other manifestation you have ever done before.

Using Vowels to Get Blissed Out in-Love

A - Align to Infinite Love

E - Embody Infinite Love

I - Intention setting as Infinite Love

O - Open fully and receive Love

U - You are the Love you seek

Y - Why, not sometimes… it's *always* been about *you*.

Call me crazy but I love that these vowels have appeared to help you successfully manifest love. All known languages have vowels and they have many uses. Not only do they give words structure but they are used to embed meaning and emotion into words. Thus allowing us to express ourselves more accurately in our communications (2, 3).

Let's do another experiment:

Out loud say "I love feeling inspired". Now add emphasis to 'love' as you say it again "I *love* feeling inspired". As you dragged out 'love' not only does your listener get a deeper understanding of how much you love being inspired but you also *feel* it within you, correct? Do it again and see for yourself by dragging out 'love' even longer. "I *looove* feeling inspired".

Feelings of 'Love' literally come alive within you as you say it.

Therefore:

Vowels are to words, what energy embodiment is to manifestation. They become *alive* and *empowered* by our emotions, our *energy*.

Incredible right? Plus the closeness in sound of 'vowels' to 'vows' can not be a coincidence!

So I set this intention for you:

May these vowels lead you to a place where you and your soulmate make commitment vows of everlasting love to each other, create the most wonderful Love Life together, where you always grow closer and more devoted to each other as each year passes.

And so it is.

A - ALIGN TO INFINITE LOVE

ALIGNMENT: Understanding the concepts and details of Infinite Love and igniting how you want Love to feel.

Deep within you, you know the feelings of being loved, and most specifically, being IN-LOVE! Those uncontainable feelings where you can't stop smiling and the whole world seems amazingly beautiful and wonderful. No problem is too big and *everything* is possible. In fact everything feels like it is overflowing with potential, just waiting to burst out.

Where you feel like you are walking on air and nothing can bring you down.

Where you radiate happiness and joy and you just can't stop smiling.

Where you feel inspired and so many new ideas keep coming to you.

Where you feel so incredibly happy that you want everyone to feel like this.

Where colours seem to pop and the flowers and plants are radiating happiness and hope.

Where it feels like the whole world is radiating love to you, that everything is so completely perfect and everything is exactly as it should be.

Where the smile on your face is so huge your face aches a little.

Where your heart feels like it is completely open and wider than you ever thought possible.

Where you feel you have enough love for the entire world.

Yes, those feelings. Can you feel them within you now?

Focus on your "In-Love" feelings and let yourself feel them completely. Keep adding to the feelings. Open up and access all your hopes and dreams about feeling loved. Make yourself the Love that you know you truly want. Align to that feeling.

Re-read and go over this section until you can feel yourself becoming lighter, happier, hopeful and loved.

E - EMBODYING INFINITE LOVE

EMBODIMENT: Take alignment a step further by becoming Infinite Love. Living, breathing, feeling and enjoying being Infinite Love. Every day as much as possible, until your soulmate arrives in your life.

It's okay to feel these feelings so completely, even if you don't have a partner. You magnify and strengthen your In-Love feelings when you do this. If you are cautious, it is okay. Feeling cautious is natural in the beginning. So gently press yourself forward emotionally and let yourself feel those amazing feelings of love. As much as you can. Progress forwards into more love, step by metaphorical step. Take one step forward, let yourself feel comfortable, then take another step. Soon you will allow yourself to become completely full of love.

Every time you do it, it will become easier and more complete.

Yes you do deserve to feel this good.

Next, start smiling and looking around with a loving gaze to see the perfection surrounding you. Choose to see perfection and love in all things. Choose to see things as they are, with no judgment about what is right or wrong, good or bad. Simply allow everything to be as it is and accept the perfection of everything, including people. Now you are infusing love energy into your surroundings and you are purifying your energy field by radiating unconditional love and acceptance. Beautiful, right? *Yes you are.*

Now simply open your awareness even further and realise that you are radiating and receiving love. You are flowing with Infinite, Unconditional, Everlasting Love.

You created this beautiful experience of Infinite Love. You did this, no one else.You hold all the power to give yourself love, by being Love. The more you embrace and embody love, the more you will realise you have simply returned to your natural state of being, that you *are* Love. Now your heart is truly open and love energy is constantly flowing to you and through you. Congratulations! You have just made yourself the most powerful magnet in the multiverse! It is with this amazing embodiment of In-love energy that successful Love intentions are set from.

I - INTENTION SETTING WITH INFINITE LOVE

Now that you are aligned and embodying Infinite Love, it is time to set your manifestation intentions. Imagine how you will feel with your partner by your side. Imagine what they will look like, what you will do together, how you will laugh, learn and love. You can set specifics at this time, like hugging a taller person (if you want a taller partner) or dancing together (if you want a dance partner) or looking lovingly into the young faces of your grandchildren with your beloved soulmate at your side. Let yourself feel how you will be with your soulmate. Feel all those In-Love emotions.

Allow yourself to daydream about your ideal relationship, all the little details like how nice it is to hold hands walking together, hugging after resolving a miscommunication, laughing together whilst cooking and cleaning, snuggling on the couch and making love. Holding each other as you share your deepest secrets and heart-felt dreams.

Seeing them as your best friend, traveling together and exploring the world. Sitting together discussing important matters with equal contribution, finding win-win solutions together. Seeing moments where anger and frustration are dropped and arguments are averted because mutual understanding, respect, love and genuine desire to understand each other, always brings cooperation and collaboration to the discussion. Where the desire to be kind, listening and understanding overrides the need to be right or win.

You can also manifest other aspects of your relationship like mutual respect, collaboration, joint projects, peaceful conflict resolution, financial security, sexual compatibility, abundance and ease. Imagine yourselves becoming closer and even more supportive during times of stress and crisis. See yourselves as best friends who always see the good in each other, particularly when the other can not. See yourselves being patient, kind, compassionate towards each other and excited, inspired and happy when you and/or your partner achieves goals and success.

Imagine your relationship ever expanding with Infinite Love, commitment, kindness, joy, abundance, inspiration, hope, contentment and peace.

Now start writing all of it down. It doesn't have to be perfect, have punctuation or even be in sentences but start channeling all your intentions onto the page. Include all your emotions and how you will both feel. Include everything you want. It can be as long as you want. Just keep your In-love feelings flowing within you. It's ok to cry tears of joy and happiness as you write. The more emotional you are the better, as it holds the pure energy of hope being realised.

When you manifest with this pure energy of In-love, somewhere on this planet your soulmate will feel your pull and start making choices that will change their lives so that they will meet up with you, to bring them into your sphere of reality. Finally, I hear you sigh. Yes! Finally!

They are definitely on their way to you, one behavior choice at a time.

O - OPEN FULLY AND RECEIVE LOVE

So far you have aligned, embodied and set your intentions which really didn't take that long. Now comes the deliberate and purposeful action in your manifestation process. Before you "do" anything, your priority is to feed your energetic bonfire, your Love Signature and your Love Portal. EVERYDAY.

Most people forget this part, or they do it for a few days and if their soulmate is not knocking on their door, they start to doubt Love, the process or worse, give up.

Well that is not going to happen to you!

Firstly, please remember, timing is everything and it is not just your timing that is involved in bringing your soulmate to you. Just like you, your soulmate doesn't always make the choice that will lead them towards you. For whatever reason, they might make a choice that leads them away from you OR keeps them on hold where they are. Don't worry, the universal processes are at play already creating another choice that will bring them closer and closer to you - one behaviour choice at a time. The same applies to you. Keep trusting, just because they are not on your doorstep doesn't mean they are not on their way to you now.

Secondly, this process may take a while, weeks or even months but don't give up! When your soulmate does arrive on your doorstep, you want them to be completely ready for you. All lessons learnt and ready to create a relationship of Infinite, Everlasting love. Do you really want them half prepared? Or two-thirds prepared? No, of course not. No more 'project relationships' for you! Only True Love with your soulmate from now on. So relax and chill out. They are coming to you, it's the law - the law of attraction. And what is a couple more weeks, months or even a year compared to a whole lifetime spent together in Infinite Love?

Maintaining your embodiment of Infinite Love is easy because it feels so good! Combining it with receiving Love everyday is a fun process you can play with to keep your energy high and in the universal flow of manifestation.

So everyday, align and embody Infinite Love by living each day like your soulmate is already in your life. You can even imagine that they have already left for work, are in the shower or on a work trip. Let yourself feel loved and blissfully happy. Feel like you are the luckiest person ever (you are by the way), and you have the most amazing relationship and love life. All your dreams have come true. Now it's time to start receiving Love from all universal sources.

The receiving mindset is such a fun process to use. Essentially, believe that everything in your life has been deliberately placed before you to acknowledge and receive love. It truly has. This is not a joke! That street tree was planted just for you (acknowledge and receive); the clouds have formed that exact shape and are present in the sky to send you love (acknowledge and receive); the birdsong is sending you love (acknowledge and receive); the flowers you pass all know you and are blooming just for you (acknowledge and receive). Your car was made especially for you, the colour was created with you in mind (acknowledge and receive). All of it is for you - even the seemingly 'bad' things. It's all there to remind you that you are Love and loved. I hope you get the idea. Spread it to all areas of your life.

I recommend you receive Love all day, every day. Live in your own world of acknowledging and receiving Love. It might take a little effort in the beginning, but it is such a fun process because it truly lifts your energy into joy, gratitude and love. It's for this reason that you just might continue to do it all your life. *I know I do.*

Don't worry about telling others about it. If they are not conscious manifesters, they probably won't understand. Who cares anyway, when you are feeling so happy, smiley and loved? Others will naturally want to know your secret. Tell them if you wish, just acknowledge and receive the love that is being sent to you. Even if they call you crazy! Ultimately it's coming from a place of love and you don't need them to understand why you are so blissfully happy with life. Usually, just the fact that you are blissfully happy, is enough for your loved ones.

Naturally, keep these processes going for as long as possible. The longer you do it, the stronger the magnetic pull of your Love Portal and your Love Signature will be to your soulmate and True Love Potentials. Put reminders in your phone, sticky notes around your house, set alarms to keep you on track. Create a Loved daily schedule. Whatever works for you, *do it*.

U - YOU ARE THE LOVE YOU SEE

Hopefully a realisation has been dawning within you. Even without a partner, you are able to feel Infinite Love, feel blissfully happy and content. So much so, that if a potential partner doesn't want this level of Infinite Love, then you would let them leave your life than to compromise the love energy you hold. Sure, a partner would be nice but you no longer NEED a soulmate to feel so strongly loved and Love.

How is this possible and most importantly, what does it mean for you?

In #4, you were guided how to Open Fully and Receive Love. When you did this, you emotionally and energetically opened your heart chakra. The more you were able to open up and feel all those delicious feelings of Infinite Love and the longer you kept your heart chakra open, the more you were able to feel YOUR OWN LOVE. That's right, your own love.

Usually when people are living their lives, they don't open up their heart chakras very wide. So they don't give and receive much love as a general rule. When they are with their loved ones however, they unconsciously open up their heart chakras. They open up their hearts because they feel safe, relaxed and now that they are open, they feel loved. The more loved they feel, the more they open their hearts.

When our loved ones are preoccupied or might be a little terse towards us, our heart chakras close off a bit because it doesn't feel safe to be so open around them at that time. When they are nice and loving towards us again, we open back up.

These types of interactions have helped to create the *biggest misunderstanding* around Love that the world has ever known. Interactions such as these, have led us to believe that Love is outside of us, and is given to us by others. However, this is not correct. Remember the Law of Attraction? You can not receive something you don't already have.

When you feel loving towards another person, *you* open your heart chakra so big and wide that you feel all the Love that sits within you. It is an infinite, constant Love and it flows from you, out into the universe. Since you *are Love*, *you* overflow with Love when you open your heart this wide. It is this love that you seek.

Remember that hole that sat deep within you when you didn't feel loved? That was caused by the closing of your own heart chakra, you were not able to feel or receive your own love. Of course it didn't feel good, of course it didn't feel right. Of course you have been searching for Love. However it was never an external love that you were missing. *It was your own.*

By now you know that Infinite Love is so much more than self-love. Self-love is an important aspect of everyone's ascension journey but it is not the True Love you seek. True Love, Infinite Love is born from within your own heart. It is what you have been practicing through this book and hopefully you will continue to do so, long after you are blissfully happy.

TRUE LOVE POTENTIALS AND SOULMATES

As a result of all your amazing work thus far, especially opening up and becoming a receiver of Love, you are now very familiar with your own Love and Love Signature. Therefore, the next step in your manifestation is to start receiving potential partners and eventually your soulmate.

It's time to celebrate and truly appreciate this momentous moment in your ascension journey. Congratulations, this is very exciting!!

This manifestation journey has hopefully guided you to know what you want in your Love relationship, particularly how you want to feel. No one can make you feel anything you don't want to feel, therefore the awareness comes that it is *your* love that is the ultimate love you seek.

So give it to yourself in bucket loads, monster pickup truck loads. Whatever vessel you use doesn't matter, simply open up and enjoy the Love that flows from you.

It is from the awareness that your own love is enough, that your True Love Potentials and eventually your soulmate will arrive in your life.

Have True Love Potentials started arriving in your life and asking you out? If they haven't they soon will.

True Love Potentials are your sign that your manifestation is on track. They show up before your soulmate. They will help you reaffirm or tweak your Love Signature and learn to stand up for it when you need to.

True Love Potentials can have a similar Love Signature to you but they are *not* your soulmate. These souls truly desire a Love Signature like yours, but they are not ready yet. They are still progressing on their journey and are in a different place to you energetically.

Remember, if something isn't right, then it is not right. Don't try to make it fit, let them go with grace and gratitude.

In my experience, you will encounter a few True Love Potentials when you reach this part of your manifestation journey. Saying no to them can be hard at the time, but True Love is worth this temporary, uncomfortable experience. Besides, once your soulmate arrives, you won't be thinking about them again.

When you know and treasure the Love within you, you become incredibly powerful. You know who you are. So when it comes to potential partners, you won't be cluelessly accepting invitations from every individual who displays interest in you. Instead, you will be so grounded in who you are and the love you hold, that you will be assessing their compatibility to your Love Standard and Signature.

So start looking or feeling the Love Standards and Signatures of True Love Potentials that have (or will soon) show up in your life. That's right, you are going to be contacted, messaged, asked out, dined, wooed etc etc. If it feels right, say yes and connect with them. Discover what their Love Signature is and if it matches yours.

Please note, you are not required to have sex with anyone to determine their Love Standard and Signature compatibility. Of course, you can if you want to, but you don't *have* to. Sex can complicate things so consider putting it on hold for a while as you get to know this potential partner. Naturally there will be chemistry between you both, but you really want your heart chakra connection to be the strongest connection, not your sacral chakra or sexual energy.

If this is your soulmate, you are about to become best friends for life. Sexual attraction will come and go and come again (pun intended) during a relationship. Support, respect, connection, commitment, shared goals, friendship and intimacy will be the glue that holds you together during the difficult times when they arise. Therefore your heart-felt connection with each other is much more important than sexual attraction at this point.

WHAT TO DO WITH TRUE LOVE POTENTIALS

Have fun together and share your hopes and dreams, desires and goals. Talk and listen. Open up about what you want in a relationship, what you believe is possible. By this stage, you should be very familiar with your own Love Signature, so you will know soon enough if there is an energetic match between you.

Sometimes it might take a little while to determine what their Love Signature is: especially if you are trying to make them fit your Love Signature. Try to simply enjoy this new experience and trust that you will know if it is right or not. However once you do know they are not compatible let them go. Don't linger in a relationship with someone that is not your soulmate.

By releasing them, you strengthen and clarify your Love Standard. You are powerfully reaffirming under the Law of Attraction what you want, which in turn produces an even stronger magnetic pull to your soulmate. If you spend too much time, considering whether a True Love Potential is your soul mate or not, you might start questioning your Love Standard, compromising on small details that can have a big impact in a lifelong relationship. It will weaken your Love

Standard and your soulmate will feel less of a magnetic pull towards you. So be clear and firm and take action when you know.

Again, please don't try to make someone fit your Love Standard or your Love Signature. Either it matches incredibly well or it doesn't. Don't make it more complicated than that. If you try to make someone fit, then it creates a *project relationship* based on conditional love. True Love doesn't work that way. Either they fit incredibly well, or not at all. If you have to think about it too much to make it work, then it doesn't work. Period. Say goodbye and let them go.

> Remember: Every relationship is bringing you TOWARDS love, not away from it. So when you let them go, you step closer to where you want to be.

Hopefully you will follow this guidance and won't get too caught up with your True Love Potentials for too long.

The benefits of engaging with True Love Potentials include feeling much clearer about what you will and won't accept regarding your Love Standard and Love Signature. When you become *super* clear, any other True Love Potentials that might have been heading your way will no longer come into your sphere of reality. Thus a clear path will be laid out for your soulmate to reach you. This might seem like a 'lull' in your love life, after the recent onslaught of potential partners that have been knocking on your door.

If a lull does occur, think of it as the drum roll that is announcing the arrival of your soulmate into your life.

OHHH THIS IS MY SOULMATE

When your soulmate does arrive, you will know it very clearly. Your questions will disappear and you will laugh because you'll realise how hard you were trying to make all the previous relationships work, and you can clearly see now that they were never going to work. With your soulmate by your side, you will see all your previous relationships as essential stepping stones to get you to your soulmate. They were never your soulmate and it was your eagerness, impatience and misdirected hope that created unnecessary drama in your life. Now you know, understand the lesson, have a good laugh and let it go. You have your whole love life with your soulmate ahead of you now.

Y - WHY? IT'S ALWAYS BEEN ABOUT YOU

Why? That is the question isn't it? Why you? Why now? Why life? Why…everything?

Find somewhere to sit outside, preferable somewhere where you are either in nature or can see it. Somewhere quiet, where you won't be disturbed. Now ask the question. Why?

Simply listen for and observe the answers…

We *always* receive answers when we ask, but usually we don't always listen for the answers. The answers arrive within you on every level. Through your senses, your physical and emotional states as well as your thoughts.

Let the answers come to you. You will be surprised at the simplicity of the truth you will find. Life doesn't have to be as complicated as we make it.

Remember: Life works for you, never against you. *Always* for you.

Life is always leading you to the best version of yourself. Always giving you opportunities to choose behaviours, actions, intentions, thoughts, words, mindsets that help you know, and be, who you truly are.To discover more of yourself, to expand beyond your own self-imposed limitations and constraints.

There is a true sense of peace, calm and contentment that comes in knowing more of who you are. Knowing that you are the centre of your own sphere of reality, *the* Creator of your life.

RELATIONSHIPS OF INFINITE LOVE

Creating and maintaining a life of Infinite Love together requires regular focus and purposeful action by both partners. It is a sacred space that has been created through the combination of your beautiful energies. It is an honour and blessing to have achieved it. Treat it as such.

Remember: If you want the most amazing relationship in the world, you need to treat your partner and your relationship like they are the most amazing partner and relationship in the world.

When you and your soulmate start a relationship based on true *Unconditional Love* it is a rare and beautiful thing. It is a relationship overflowing with fifth dimensional energy of love, kindness, hope and inspiration.

When you are already radiating Infinite Love and love how you feel, your soulmate will enter your life. You will discover that they are also radiating Infinite Love. When two souls come together already carrying Infinite Love, the relationship that is created is beyond anything they could have ever imagined. Energetically the relationship births pure seventh dimensional Love frequencies onto the planet. This *Higher Love* is of a very pure vibration and frequency and yes, it feels amazing. Physically, the reality of the relationship is mutual respect, expansion, joy, happiness, love, kindness and a true desire to keep the relationship as loving and clear as possible. That means when miscommunications inevitably arise and conflict occurs, both partners work together to resolve the miscommunication together and restore their relationship connection back to its usual solidarity of unconditional love. The desire to keep the relationship as amazing as it is, will always be stronger than the pull of conflict and disagreement.

It is a relationship where both partners are deeply in Love and radiate so much Love that others will comment on how special it is, how they also desire a relationship similar to yours. The difference in your relationship will be obvious to all. They will naturally desire a relationship similar to yours because that is the light within you calling the light within them to evolve and ascend.

What a beautiful journey you planned out for yourself.

GLOSSARY

Ascension Gift

A realisation about yourself and who you can be. Usually found within pivotal moments in a relationship. Often pivotal moments can change the direction of a relationship in one of two ways. For example, due to a disagreement, a relationship can be altered with more trauma, distress and heartbreak or it can change with a new awareness of acceptance, understanding and enlightenment. Usually we get caught in the drama and the trauma which stays in that moment for many years. The ascension gift will stay there until it is found through healing work. Ascension gifts are only found through unconditional love, acceptance and contentment. You will know it when you find it, as it will unlock a joyous awareness within you that enlightens your wisdom and propels you forwards on your ascension journey.

Everlasting Love

Infinite Love that is particularly shared between two soulmates. It denotes that they have been soulmates together in previous lifetimes and experiences, on this planet and on others, in physical realms and non-physical realms. Not always in the same gender or even in physical forms. It is a deep loving bond that once formed can never be forgotten, even when they do not choose to be each other's soulmates in a lifetime.

Infinite Love

The type of Love or energy that creates universes. It is constant, everflowing, unrestricted, in all things, flowing in and out of all things, ever expanding and never ending, hence the name: infinite.

In-Love

A short form of Infinite Love. In-Love feels like those feelings you feel when you are first in Love. Most people are familiar with these feelings from the beginning of new relationships. It is generally believed that this new love feeling won't last and fade away after a few months or years. Well you have just proved them wrong, haven't you? You don't even need a relationship to feel them. So how long you feel them is truly up to you.

Love Standard

Is a clear picture or a clearer emotional understanding of your best love life with your soulmate and sets a benchmark of the type of Love you will accept in your life moving forward. A commitment to your Love Standard is a firm intention that you will only accept potential partners who resonate with this purity of love or higher. It is felt right throughout the multiverses.

Love Signature

Your Love Signature is similar to an energetic pulse that you are constantly emitting out across the multiverses. It carries information about your entire energetic vibration and frequency and in particular, your Love vibration. It signals to potential partners all your desires, hopes, dreams, fears and doubts you hold regarding love and the life you hope to create with your partner. Only vibrational matches to your Love Signature will be triggered by it and will move towards you both energetically and physically. Whatever energy you hold, you will attract its vibrational match into your life.

Sphere of Reality

Your life. Your everyday experience of life including the things around you in the physical world and within you in your energetic world and beyond.

True Love Potentials

Potential romantic partners that show up in your life, especially when you are manifesting your soulmate. True Love Potentials are drawn to you because they truly desire your Love Standard and Signature, however they have not reached that in their life yet. You are helping them understand what they truly want in their romantic relationships and they are helping you reaffirm your Love Standard and Signature. They are not your soulmate, but they might feel like they *could* be one day.

BIBLIOGRAPHY

1. DiGiuseppe, R., David, D., & Venezia, R. (2016). Cognitive theories. In J. C. Norcross, G. R. VandenBos, D. K. Freedheim, & B. O. Olatunji (Eds.), *APA handbook of clinical psychology: Theory and research* (pp.145–182). American Psychological Association. https://doi.org/10.1037/14773-006

2. https://www.ncbi.nlm.nih.gov/pmc/articles/PMC3292616/#:~:text=Vow els%20are%20also%20the%20primary,the%20word%20%E2%80%9Cp resent%E2%80%9D). April 13, 2024

3. https://pbsi-upr.id/index.php/atmosfer/article/download/230/193#:~:text=%2D%20 Vowels%3A%20Vowels%20form%20the%20core,words%2C%20and% 20role%20in%20communication. April 13, 2024